This Big Hill

By Sally Cowan

Pop and I go up this big hill.

We look at the big ants.

The ants run on the moss.

Then, we look at bugs that buzz and buzz on little buds.

Buzz! Buzz!

We get up to the top.

We can see a lot at the cliff.

We can see ships in the sun.

But then the fog comes in.

We can not see the ships.

Pop and I can see big gulls.

They sit on that cliff.

Some gulls have red legs.

They can get cod and scoff them up.

Pop got a photo of this little gull.

A shop is on the hill.

This shop sells buns.

Pop likes to scoff them!

Yum! Yum!

Pop and I have lots of fun on this big hill.

CHECKING FOR MEANING

1. Where did Pop and the boy see ants running? *(Literal)*

2. What did Pop and the boy see at the top of the cliff? *(Literal)*

3. How would the gulls get the cod? *(Inferential)*

EXTENDING VOCABULARY

then	Look at the word *then*. What is the initial sound in this word? Find another word in the book that has the same sound at the start of the word.
they	Look at the word *moss*. Moss is a plant that does not have flowers. It grows in damp, wet places. Can you think of other animals that might walk or run on moss?
photo	What can we use to take a photo? Is *photo* a short form of a longer word? What is the longer word?

MOVING BEYOND THE TEXT

1. What do you enjoy doing with your pop or gran?

2. Why do some children spend lots of time with their grandparents?

3. Have you been on a nature walk? What did you see? Who went with you?

4. Why do you think the shop on the hill sells food?

SPEED SOUNDS

| sh | ch | th | th | wh | qu | ph |

voiced   unvoiced

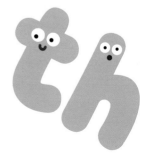

PRACTICE WORDS

Then

this

that

ships

This

shop

them